# 40 Years of Miracles

## By
## Rodney Oxbrow

Copyright © 2024 Rodney Oxbrow

ISBN: 978-1-917129-48-0

All rights reserved, including the right to reproduce this book, or portions thereof in any form. No part of this text may be reproduced, transmitted, downloaded, decompiled, reverse engineered, or stored, in any form or introduced into any information storage and retrieval system, in any form or by any means, whether electronic or mechanical without the express written permission of the author.

Contents

Preface
Chapter One. When I didn't know Him.
Chapter Two. 100 years old and regaining sight.
Chapter Three. Witnessing a leg grow in front of my eyes.
Chapter Four. Selling the apartment in Northolt.
Chapter Five. RV World and a bank in Dallas.
Chapter Six. Meeting Marvin Baker.
Chapter Seven. The trip to Laredo.
Chapter Eight. The washing machine man.
Chapter Nine. The lady with terminal cancer.
Chapter Ten. Linda Summers.
Chapter Eleven. The Little guy.
Chapter Twelve. The electric bill.
Chapter Thirteen. Jessie Rocha.
Chapter Fourteen. The Synagogue in Dallas.
Chapter Fifteen. Two £5 notes.
Chapter Sixteen. The Ira.
Chapter Seventeen. Looking for my Father.
Chapter Eighteen. The beach in Australia.
Conclusion.

# Preface

## A Miracle

***"An extraordinary occurrence that surpasses all known human powers or natural forces and is as cribed to a divine or supernatural cause, esp. to God."***

Today, at the time of drafting this book, I am 74 years old and have been a Christian walking with the Lord for over 40 years. During all those years, I have seen God move in incredible ways. Sometimes, they have been stunning miracles that happen right in front of your eyes, like seeing a leg grow; other times, you just experience something so exceptional that it could only be a God-incidence, not a coincidence.

In the following chapters, I have shared many of the experiences I have enjoyed in 40-plus years, however, there are more things that I have seen and experienced than I can recall or write down. The last verse in the book of John (John 21:25) reads, "And there are also many other things that Jesus did, which if they were written one by one, I suppose that even the world itself could not contain the books that would be written. Amen."

I am in no way comparing myself to Jesus. It is just that when you recognize God's involvement in your life, it is easy to see how wonderful He is. The average person couldn't look back over their life and remember all the wonderful little acts of love that their earthly father did while they were growing up. It is no different for a Christian to look back over their life and see how their Heavenly Father has loved, provided, and protected them also.

I am blessed to be able to share just a few of the things my Heavenly Father has done in my life. I hope it encourages you and proves to be a blessing to you.

# Chapter One

## Even When I Didn't Know Him

Looking back at my childhood, I see signs that His hand was upon my life. Without delving too much into my background, it suffices to say that we were poor. My mother, Betty, and two older half-brothers were my family, residing in a two-bedroom house in Luton, Bedfordshire. At the age of 8, I began experiencing excruciating back pain, an ordeal uncommon for a child of my age.

My mother took me to our family doctor, a tall, thin German man named Dr. Lowery, who, with his towering height of about 6ft 6 inches, my mother was 4ft 10 inches, reassured my mother that the pain was due to rheumatism. I cannot recall if any remedy was given, but several weeks later, we found ourselves back with Dr. Lowery, who once again attributed the pain to rheumatism.

Fortunately, my mother decided to seek a second opinion from a different doctor, Dr. Graham, a Scottish man. After examining me and conducting urine tests, Dr. Graham diagnosed a serious kidney disease, leading to three years away from school. Prior to this, I had been a choir boy at St. Matthews C of E church and attended St. Matthews Church of England school, where lessons about Jesus were a weekly occurrence – a practice long gone unfortunately.

This experience laid the foundation of my faith. Despite life's ups and downs, I never once doubted the existence of God and the miraculous events surrounding Jesus during His time on earth. However, God, to me, seemed distant, residing 100 million miles away in heaven, with little influence on my life or acknowledgement of my existence.

I believed that I would join Him in heaven upon death, but that was the extent of it. I knew about Him but did not truly know Him or believe that such knowledge was attainable before my eventual demise.

As the years passed, I encountered the various facets of life, both positive and negative, until I found myself at the age of 33, no longer desiring to live. Divorce had separated me from my first wife and two-year-old son, Timothy. Simultaneously, I faced bankruptcy. Filled with despair, I contemplated ending my life.

During the day, I portrayed a façade of positivity as Mr. Motivation in my role in the insurance industry, overseeing a team of young professionals. However, internally, I longed for death. Reflecting on Matthew 23:27-28, where Jesus likened the Pharisees to whitewashed tombs, beautiful on the outside but concealing decay within, I felt akin to this metaphor, hiding my inner struggles behind a cheerful exterior.

Having secluded myself in a bed-sitting room in North London for about six weeks when not working, I planned to end my life without anyone knowing or intervening.

The fateful Saturday arrived, and I spent three hours composing a detailed suicide note. Listing instructions about my £153 worth of premium bonds, the recipient of my guitar, and my desired funeral arrangements, I was indulging in a self-pitying exercise but was deadly serious about taking my life.

Placing the finished letter in an envelope addressed to Peter Deane, a work colleague and close friend unaware of my address, I laid it on the small sideboard in the room. I sat on the edge of the bed, contemplating the final moments before taking my own life when an unexpected knock on the door interrupted my thoughts.

Anticipating Jehovah Witnesses, I reluctantly opened the door to find Peter Deane standing there, unaware of my address. Stunned, I asked, "Oh, Hi Pete, what are you doing here?" His response left me in shock: "God has sent me round. He said that you are going to kill yourself and that you should give Him your life. He will give it back to you with so much more."

In that moment, I realized that God was not distant but intimately concerned about me. Peter urged me to gather my belongings and immediately move in with him and Claire, his partner, an intervention that marked a significant turning point in my life. Over the following months, I regained strength under their support.

One day, while reading a magazine, I came across an advertisement for a free book called "Power for Living." Intrigued, I requested the book, which arrived two weeks later. Unable to put it down, I read testimonies from well-known Christians like Cliff Richards and Susie Sainsbury until I reached page 63.

On that page, readers were invited to pray a prayer of salvation, asking God for His eternal life and the indwelling of the Holy Spirit. I prayed this prayer, not fully comprehending its impact, closed the book, and drifted off to sleep.

Upon awakening, an urgent desire to acquire a Bible consumed me. Fuelled by this burning need, I walked from my office in Victoria to Westminster Cathedral's bookshop. Inside, a nun approached me, suggesting that I didn't need a Bible but only the sacraments. Recognizing the disparity between man-made Catholicism and a genuine spiritual relationship with God, I opted for a Good News Bible from WH Smith as a starting point.

In Matthew 13:31-35, Jesus used the metaphor of a mustard seed to illustrate the Kingdom of God, emphasizing the potential for growth in our lives. That seed had been planted, and from that day forward, it began to grow and grow.

# Chapter Two

## One Hundred Years Old and Regaining Sight

Over the next two years, my life moved forward. I found myself running a small insurance brokerage in London, no longer working with Peter. A young man named Steve Turner joined my company, and he invited me to his church one Sunday. Despite its location on the other side of London from where I lived, I decided to attend the following Sunday.

The Open-Door Community church convened in a small hall in Uxbridge, boasting a congregation of about 45 people. Initially, I thought they were all eccentric; hands raised high in song. I must have appeared awkward, standing like a statue while everyone else danced and sang with radiant smiles on their faces.

Among them was a blonde woman who kept dancing back and forth in the aisle, smiling as she passed me. After the service, amidst more singing and dancing, Steve Turner introduced me to this woman, Susan Kincaid, whom he referred to as his spiritual mother.

Susan, about my age, introduced me to her son, Clayton, who was 18 at the time. They both seemed genuinely pleasant, and Susan and I found ourselves married six weeks later. The six weeks leading to our wedding were filled with divine experiences that could fill a book on their own.

It was an exhilarating time for us both. What made it even more special was our shared musical talents—I played the piano and guitar proficiently, while Susan was an excellent lyricist. Together, we began composing Christian songs, one of which, "I See Jesus," we performed for 240 people at our wedding.

A friend gifted us a two-week holiday in Cornwall, which was a delightful wedding present. During one sunny drive along the country lanes near our lodging, Susan suddenly exclaimed, "Rod, stop! I believe the Lord has directed us to pray with that old lady at that house." I admitted I hadn't even noticed a house, let alone an old lady. Nevertheless, I halted the car and reversed about 50 yards. As rain suddenly poured down, Susan eagerly stepped out of the car and made her way up the steep driveway toward the old lady who had begun to rise from her deck chair because of the rain.

Having recently witnessed God's power in various ways, I decided to emulate Jesus and take control of the weather. I rebuked the rain in Jesus' name, and to my amazement, it ceased as swiftly as it had begun. I followed Susan up the driveway, where we found the old lady, wearing dark glasses and appearing frail. Susan cheerfully greeted her and expressed our intention to pray with her. The old lady responded, "Oh, how lovely of you. Jesus has been my overcoat all my life. I am 100 years old, and He has just given me my sight back." At that moment, a woman emerged from the house, inquiring about our presence, Susan explained, mentioning the old lady's kindness. The woman replied, "Well, if she's that lovely, you can take her with you."

The old lady explained, "That's Gladys my daughter, don't mind her; she doesn't know Jesus." We prayed for the old lady, bid our farewells, and departed. Such encounters were commonplace for Susan, but for me, it was a glowing moment of joy. I'm not implying that our prayer restored her sight; rather, it was the divine inspiration behind the event itself.

Our honeymoon in Cornwall was eventful; getting to know someone so quickly isn't easy. Alongside the wonderful moments, which included ministering with three of our songs in a Christian tent meeting with 350 attendees, we also faced challenges. I anticipated the occasional friction as we both had prior marriages, but it escalated physically, given Susan's strength and firmness of character.

# Chapter Three

## Witnessing a leg grow in front of my eyes

The Open-Door church experienced remarkable growth over the next year, much of it owing to Susan's evangelism efforts and our commitment to bring newcomers to church each Sunday. One of the esteemed elders, Weldon, whom I deeply admired, handed me a tape one day. It featured the testimony of a remarkable man named Jim Sepulvida, who has since passed away. I cherished the tape, listening to it at least four times before returning it to Weldon.

Jim's testimony recounted his miraculous healing by God and subsequent mission to heal others worldwide. About a month later, Weldon approached me at church, bubbling with excitement. Jim Sepulvida was visiting England, hosting a special breakfast at a hotel on the outskirts of London, and Weldon had secured tickets for us both.

On the appointed Saturday, we arrived promptly for the 7:00 am breakfast. Jim's entrance into the room electrified the atmosphere. After breakfast, Jim announced a time of ministry. As the waitresses cleared plates, Jim approached one and asked for a moment of her time.

He informed her that God has revealed to him, that she had one leg shorter than the other and offered to pray for her healing. Though taken aback, she consented. Jim placed a chair in an open area, covering her legs with a tea towel for modesty. The difference in length was apparent.

Jim assured her that God would perform a miracle without physical contact. We watched in awe as, following a moment of prayer, her shorter leg began to grow until it passed the other leg, and then the other leg started to grow until both were equal in length. It was an unexpected and miraculous sight, leaving us all astonished, including the waitresses, one of whom shed tears of joy and wonder. This wasn't just a story confined to ancient times in the Bible, but a modern-day miracle unfolding before us.

Later that evening, Susan and I attended Jim's healing meeting at a local hall. With a simple stage set-up and local musicians leading worship, Jim shared his testimony before inviting individuals forward for prayer. Without physical touch, he spoke gently, and individuals would collapse as they were being touched by the Holy Spirit.

It was a day of extraordinary experiences, and I urge anyone reading this to seek out Jim's testimony on-line—it will undoubtedly inspire and uplift you.

# Chapter Four

## Selling the Apartment in Northolt

Susan and I continued to write Christian songs and were being asked quite often to minister in different churches. I would play the guitar, and Susan would be the main singer, with me harmonizing. Susan also had a job with the local Hillingdon council, helping the long-term unemployed back into the workplace. She was busy with appointments every day, going to different unemployment benefit offices.

However, for almost a whole week, hardly anyone came in for an appointment, which left Susan just sitting at a desk with nothing to do for long periods of time, this was very rare. Suddenly, first thing on the Monday morning, she started to get words coming into her head. She would pick up a pen and paper and found that she was writing incredible words down faster than she could think about them. Things like this called "Why should I be different?" depicted a young man walking along the road who is approached by someone giving out Christian tracts.

*Why should I be different, I like this life of mine,*
*I like to do what I want to; hey everything is fine.*
*Oh sure, I know the world is rough, but I get by okay,*
*Some people need to have something to get them through the day.*
*But me? I don't need a crutch, religion? Who needs that?*
*Don't give me all this Jesus stuff, come on it's all old hat.*
*But if it keeps you happy, well that's all well and good,*

*But listen, I'm not interested is that understood?*
*Okay, okay, I'll take the book, but don't give me all this jive,*
*What do you mean I'm dead in sin, well how come you're alive?*
*Oh, hold it now, what did I say? I've opened up a door,*
*I asked a stupid question, now you're gonna tell me more.*
*Okay okay I'll listen, but don't expect a sale,*
*Round here I'm known as tough you know,*
*They've all tried, but they fail.*
*Whoaa, what's happening here? I'm getting warm inside,*
*I'm being drained of arrogance, hey, watch out there goes pride.*
*I really can't believe this, I'm here purely for the ride,*
*Well bless my soul, I'm feeling whole,*
*So, this is why Christ died.*

And here is another one. This is about a young girl, 14 or 15 years of age who is obviously in despair.

*I know I'm always doing things that really leave me cold.*
*I know that I get on by acting tough.*
*And there really isn't any need to be quite so loud and bold,*
*But I always was the last to say, enough!*
*There's an emptiness inside me that I've tried so hard to fill,*
*I've tried drugs and alcohol. But it's still there.*
*Then my mother got a brainwave and she put me on the pill,*
*And sex became available to share.*
*Only sharing wasn't quite the way it worked out,*
*I mean, sharing means you give as well as take.*
*And I never really knew what it was all about,*
*And now I realise …..it's all a fake.*
*It's not the way I imagined love to be,*

*Everything's so easy, but no fun.*
*And oh. it's just so hard to stop self-hatred filling me,*
*I look around, there's just no place to run.*
*I thought parents were supposed to bring us up to walk a straight road,*
*Surely, they're the ones that we look to.*
*Shouldn't they be teaching us some sort of moral code?*
*I mean, here we are not sure of what to do….*
*So, we follow with the crowd and get sucked into the stream,*
*And we travel on a steady downward trend...*
*Isn't anybody out there understanding what I mean?*
*And oh, God, will this hurting in me never end?*
*There's desperation in my soul, I want to end my life,*
*It's not an idle threat, I'll make them sorry.*
*There's confusion in my brain and my thoughts are running rife,*
*And an urgency inside that bids me hurry.*
*In the drawer beside Mum's bed. There's a bottle.*
*Sleeping pills I think, I'll take them all.*
*Oh God, I'm so desperately unhappy,*
*Isn't anybody there to hear me call……..*
*I don't want to die; I don't want to die……Please.*

All these words were awesome and seemed to address topics that were going on inside people's hearts but not necessarily things spoken out. Over that week, God had given Susan pages and pages of insightful verses which seemed to go hand in hand with the songs that we had written.

It came to our minds that we had the makings of a Christian musical called "The Vineyard". Also, we both felt that God was calling us to go to America with the musical, which had its own excitements and problems alike.

One of the things that had to be done was to either sell or rent out our flat in Northolt. I made a phone call to a local estate agent, and it was arranged that the agent would come and have a look at the apartment the following day.
Sure enough, I looked out of the window at 11 a.m. and saw Mr. Williams having a good look at the building from the outside. A few minutes later, he knocked on the door, introduced himself, and proceeded to carry out an assessment of the inside.

After about 10 minutes, he said that he had assessed everything, that it was a nice flat, and that we shouldn't have a problem selling it for £46, £47, or maybe even £48,000. I explained to Mr. Williams that we hadn't yet decided if we were going to sell the flat or rent it out while we were away, but that we would pray about it and get back to him sometime soon.

Susan and I talked about it that evening, and we both felt very confident that we were meant to sell the flat, so the only question was how much for. Clayton had decided that he would come with us to the US, and we had booked for us all to leave on the 21st of July 1987. We decided on that date as we wanted to go to a particular Christian convention in the Tarrant County Convention Centre in Fort Worth, Texas, and that seemed the correct day for us to be able to be there and get settled for a day or two first. However, it was the beginning of May, so things needed to get moving quickly.

When I woke up the next morning, I knew that God was telling me that we should sell the flat for £53,000, which was a lot more than Mr. Williams said the going rate was for a flat like ours in that area. However, I was certain that I had heard God tell me the amount.

I called Mr. Williams just after 9:00 that morning to tell him that we had decided to sell and not let it out for rent while abroad, and we fixed a time for the following day for him to come back, take photographs of the flat, and sign some forms.

Mr. Williams turned up as expected, taking many photos of the outside and many of the inside too. A few minutes later, we both sat down in the kitchen to discuss things while drinking our tea. Before we discussed anything about the flat, I took that opportunity to tell him about Jesus and what God had done in our lives. Mr. Williams was very stoic as he assured me that because he went to a C of E church, he was OK but appreciated all that I was saying.

"Now, Mr. Oxbrow, what did you and Mrs. Oxbrow decide on? The £46, £47, or are you going to hope for £48,000?" I assured him that I had heard from God, and that He had told me to put it on the market for £53,000. Well, the look on Mr. Williams' face was classic.

"£53,000, Mr. Oxbrow? That is quite a lot more than the going rate. I have been in this business for over 25 years, Mr. Oxbrow, and I know this business very, very well, and I don't think you will be able to sell it for that amount. Still, you have a little bit of time left before you

HAVE to sell it, so you can always lower the price to find a buyer, can't you."

He finished his tea, bid me farewell, assuring me that he would put the flat on the market that afternoon and that he would be in touch sometime soon with an update and to see if we wanted to lower the price.

I thanked him and said my goodbye feeling confident that I had started the process and that it was now down to God to bring a buyer in. The phone rang about 2:30 pm, and Mr. Williams was on the other end. "Mr. Oxbrow, I can't believe this, I have someone who wants to buy your flat and they have agreed to pay the £53,000. Now I have been in this business for over 25 years, Mr. Oxbrow, and I've never seen anything like this."

It turned out to be two people who had a contract at the Hoover building not far away and needed a two-bedroom flat near the tube station.

What was great, the lady, one of the couple's father, was a solicitor and wanted to get it all sorted out ASAP, so we were suddenly going to be homeless far earlier than expected. It all went through as anticipated, and dear friends had a spare room for Susan and I to live in for the 6 weeks until departure day. Clayton went and stayed with one of his friends so that was another problem solved.

We decided to give all our furniture and belongings away rather than sell them and hired a van for a day to achieve this. There were many people in our church that had very little in the way of furniture. One guy had not long come out of prison prior to becoming a Christian, and we had great pleasure in kitting his place out and giving our stereo system to another and so on. It was a wonderful experience. Every time we gave something away, it was as if a string had been cut that had been binding us and then setting us free.

July 21st arrived, and Susan, Clayton, and I, two guitars, and a banker's draft for £17,500 left Gatwick for Dallas, Texas, and a whole new adventure.

# Chapter Five

## RV World, and a bank in Dallas

We arrived at DFW airport all excited but without much of an idea of what to do or where to go, other than heading for Fort Worth, about 70 miles from Dallas because of the convention. It was the height of summer, so when we collected our things off the baggage carousel, we joined the back of the line of 350 or more people all waiting to go through the immigration check-in. At the speed people were moving, we wouldn't be through for at least an hour to an hour and a half, which was a pain.

An official-looking guy was walking past the line of people, and much to Susan and Clayton's annoyance, I asked if we had to declare the fact that we effectively had an amount of money that had to be declared. With Susan looking at me with daggers because she thought that we were going to be detained for even longer than the hour and a half, we as a family followed this man to an office where I had to sign a declaration regarding the banker's draft. That done, he opened a door, and we were suddenly on the outside of the airport, not back at the rear of the queue.

I didn't have to say anything to Susan or Clayton, but I must admit I had a smile on my face that said it all, as once again scripture came to mind. "The last shall be first and the first shall be last," Matthew 19:30

We went back inside the airport and hired a big car, we decided on a Crown Victoria, which is like a big FBI car. We needed a big car as we each had a big suitcase, plus two guitars in their cases and all the hand luggage. Once again, we saw God move incredibly in just over a ten-minute period at the Avis desk while waiting our turn in the queue. The price of hiring the Crown Victoria went down three times in that time; even the guy behind the desk couldn't believe it. It suddenly became as cheap as hiring a small compact car.

We felt so good driving on the Loop 820 toward Fort Worth; we just knew that God was in control of everything and that we could relax and see what He had in store next for us. Just prior to leaving England, an American guy from Texas who was a member of our church said when you get to the US, look for a Motel 6; they are quite good value for you to stay in until you get yourselves settled and they all have a pool. However, about a week before we left the UK, I thought it would be a good idea to buy a motor-home and live in that while we decided where to settle. That way, we could see Texas and visit family or friends from church who lived in Laredo and other places we wanted to see. Susan and Clayton liked the idea too, so that was another thing on the agenda.

As we started to enter the outskirts of Fort Worth, we could sense just how big this place was. Dallas has a metroplex area that incorporates many towns and cities from around 100 miles around the city of Dallas itself. Fort Worth is one of the cities, but it isn't like a city in the UK; this was very large indeed, and we could see the many tall buildings in the centre from miles out. "Look …..there's a sign for a Motel 6." Clayton was right;

sure enough, up on the right-hand side there was a Motel 6, and we were checked into the room and in the outside pool all within 15 minutes. It was about 3:30 pm and 107 degrees Fahrenheit, so the pool was really needed; us poor English people were not used to this kind of heat.

A little later in the afternoon, we decided to leave the Motel 6 and go look around the area at motor-homes, as well as finding a restaurant to eat dinner, our first meal in the US. So, we got in our FBI car and drove along Airport Free-way for about half a mile and could see a large RV dealership on the right-hand side of the road called RV World.

We pulled into the driveway hoping the place might be open, but the gates were closed unfortunately; however, we could see a number of motor-homes from outside the gates anyway, so we got a taste of what they were like. "Hi, can I help you folks"? His name was Bill, and we explained who we were and what we were interested in. Bill took our details down and gave us Marvin Baker's phone number; Marvin was the owner and out of town for two days.

We thanked Bill, got back in the car, and drove around until we found a restaurant we liked the look of, had dinner, and then retired back to the motel and slept as it had been a very long day.

The next day was to be a trip into Dallas itself. Our banker's draft was made out to Bank of America, Dallas. No address and nothing to go on, but it should be ok, how hard could it be? We set off on Loop 820 again toward Dallas, which was about 70 miles away from Fort Worth.

About half an hour along the road, we could suddenly see the tops of the skyscrapers many miles away. The nearer we got to Dallas, the bigger it became; it was massive, and so much bigger than the centre of London.

When we entered the city, we drove around for quite a long time hoping to see the Bank of America somewhere, but without success. So, we decided to park up the car in one of the many street-level parking lots for $3 and catch a bus or walk until we managed to find the bank. So, I drove into the very next parking lot we came across, and a big guy came up to the window of the car for the money. I gave him a $5 note, and as he gave me the change, I asked him if he happened to know where the Bank of America was in Dallas. He stood up straight, pointed to the massive skyscraper behind him, and said, "Hey mister, you're in their car park." God had done it again. It may not come across to the reader just how amazing this was, but if you can imagine coming to London from a different country, going to Oxford Street and asking a salesman in some shop if he knows someone called Peter Johnson and the guy says that he is Peter Johnson, it was that unique.

# Chapter Six

## Meeting Marvin Baker

The following day, back at Motel 6, eagerly anticipating the convention set to commence in Fort Worth in three days' time. Once again, we ventured out of the motel to find somewhere to have lunch, and while we were out, I decided to call Marvin Baker, the owner of the Recreational Vehicle dealership. We spoke on the phone and arranged to meet at RV World the following day.

The next day, we drove into the massive reception parking area of RV World and were greeted by a very elegant, beautiful, woman with an amazing hairstyle. She welcomed us with a beaming smile in typical Texan fashion, saying, "Well Hi, you must be the Oxbrows. Well, just come on in and meet Micky. My name is Twilight." As we found out a few minutes later, Marvin was called Micky by close friends and family.

We followed this bubbly lady, who turned out to be Mrs. Baker, Micky's wife, into a very nice, typical Texan office—lots of wood and a massive desk, just like you see on TV but without the dead animal hanging on the wall. I don't know what I expected Micky to be like, probably 6ft 6 inches tall and 220 lbs. This is not how Micky was; he was about 5ft 10, and his frame matched his height.

I liked him immediately; he was very warm and greeted us like long-lost friends. Susan and I sat down, and Clayton stood behind us as I introduced each of us to him, and he did the same with himself, while Twilight stood behind Micky.

He asked what we were doing in Fort Worth, and we explained that we were there for the Christian convention starting Monday. He told us that Twilight was a Christian, and that he was Jewish, and then proceeded to tell us about the members of his family. They had a daughter called Misty Dawn, another daughter called Tina Star, Twilight Dew had a brother called Sunset Ray, and they also had a son called Jeremy.

This was all very well, but I wanted to talk about motor-homes and hopefully sit in one or even drive one. However, Micky kept on about the UK and the time he came over and visited a castle. Every time I got us back on the motor-home topic, he changed it back to families. I happened to mention that it must be nice to have three children, and that in the UK most families have one, maybe two children, and that it is not often you hear of large families in the UK.

"Although our pastor's brother has 6 children," I said, "which is more than practically anyone in England." "Twilight, what was the name of that English Pastor who stayed with us last year, he had six children?" "Jonathan Edwards, dear," "our pastor's brother is also called Jonathan Edwards," I said......... as we all suddenly realized that it was the same Jonathan Edwards. We were all totally stunned at the realization that God had brought us all together out of 300+ million people.

We did get to discuss buying a motor-home, but not before he insisted that we check out of Motel 6 and move into their home until we get a motor-home, their children apart from Misty Dawn were all away at camp for another four weeks.

He also said that we should give the FBI car back, as he had a Cadillac that I could use until he found us a motor-home. God had done it again; only our third day in the US and we had seen Him move already in powerful ways. We did move in with Micky and Twilight and their little 4-year-old princess Misty Dawn, and enjoyed driving around in a beautiful Cadillac for about three weeks until Micky managed to get us a 26ft Diplomat motor-home, which was just what we needed.

# Chapter Seven

## The Trip to Laredo

The motor-home was wonderful to drive and easy to live in. It easily slept six if needed, had cruise control, a toilet, a shower, microwave, and even a crystal chandelier. We had a few days away from Micky and Twilight to get used to being in the motor-home, but then we were ready to go travelling. The next stop was Laredo, about 430 miles from Dallas, and in a motor-home, it was expected to take about 8.5 hours.

We set off on the journey going via Houston as we wanted to visit a particular church there. However, we arrived in Houston late at night and stayed in a Catholic school car park, leaving first thing at 6 am to get out of the city as we didn't feel safe in that place.

Between Houston and Laredo, there was a long road right through the desert, like in all the cowboy films, rarely seeing another vehicle just cactus. Having left Houston, we were pleased that we were over halfway to Laredo and would hopefully be there before nightfall.

Everything was good: Susan was sitting in one of the armchairs reading the Bible, and Clayton was conked out, lying on his bed. It was so nice cruising along on the open road at 50 miles an hour without a care in the world, letting the cruise control do all the work as it was a totally straight road for miles and miles, and I could relax and just steer, or so I thought. Suddenly, we started to increase in speed from 50 to 55, then 56-57-60, and now it was serious.

The brakes would not slow it down adequately, and the cruise control had jammed open. The motor-home was now rocking from side to side, and we were now doing 65 mph. Susan had put the Bible down, and she and Clayton started to pray out loud. There was a horrible burning smell as I kept applying the brakes. What would become of us? Would the vehicle just keep getting faster and faster until we turned over and caught fire? Who knows! It was now getting desperate, and near 70 mph, everything in the motor-home was flying around, plates and cups, etc. getting smashed, books and papers all ending up on the floor.

I still don't know how it happened, but somehow (God) managed to get the speed down to 65, then 60, 55, 50, and although it was like trying to harness a bronco or catch a massive swordfish, somehow, I managed to bring the vehicle to a stop. The engine was still running, although I had taken the keys out. It was revving loudly, then a backfire, then more high revving followed by more backfires, and although I had taken the keys out and stopped the fuel supply, it was still going. The three of us were just standing outside looking at it, as it continued to backfire and seeming to have a life on its own.

A car did come along the road from Laredo, and the driver got out to see if he could help and said that he had never ever heard of this happening before. I don't believe I'm being Super Spiritual when I say this, but it really did feel that we were under attack spiritually. Lots of wonderful things happened in Laredo like Susan and I ministering to a married couple who were about to break up and get a divorce until God used us to speak into their lives, among other things that happened. So, looking back as we did, it really did seem that the evil one didn't want us to get to Laredo.

Anyway, we let the motor-home cool down for an hour or so before setting off for the remainder of the journey, which went off without a hitch, I'm pleased to say. We carried on to Laredo because we were expected at George and Elsie Lonchar's house that evening; they were the parents of the young guy in our old church who told us about Motel 6. We arrived at their home in Laredo early evening and were greeted so warmly by George and Elsie it made the trip well worth while. We planned to stay down in the area for a week or so, allowing time to go and minister in their church which had already been arranged.

# Chapter Eight

## The Washing Machine Man

We arrived sometime early in the evening at George and Elsie's place in Laredo, had a lovely Tex-Mex meal, spent some fellowship time, and then went to our rooms. When we woke up in the morning, George had already gone off to work, so I sat and played on their piano while Susan, Clayton, and Elsie sat in the kitchen talking.

Sometime during that period, the doorbell rang, and Elsie said in her broken Mexican/American accent, "Oh, that will be the man to fix the washing machine." I don't know why, but we all went to the door to see who it was, and sure enough, it was a Mexican man standing there with his bag of tools. She greeted him in Spanish, explaining, I think, why she had an entourage to look at the washing machine. We all left the house and walked along the side of the house to the big double garage where the washing machine was kept. Elsie opened the door of the garage to reveal a very large top-loading washing machine, much bigger than anything we get to see in the UK.

The man looked at the machine, lifting the top to reveal a washing machine full of dirty washing and dirty water. He spent a few minutes checking this and that and trying all sorts of things, but without success. Finally, he said in English, "It's no good, Elsie. You need a new motor, and it's not worth replacing it; you might as well buy a new machine."

We all stood there for 30 seconds or so, and then I said, "Let's see what God says about this." Very bold of me, I know, but I stepped forward, put my hands in the water, grabbing hold of the spindle part in the middle of all the water, commanding it to start working as it was designed to do in Jesus' name, and to everyone's amazement, including mine, it started to work.

Everyone's eyes were wide open, staring at the washing machine that was dead a few seconds earlier. Susan, Clayton, and I walked back into the house, with me obviously glowing because I had just done a miracle. No, only joking, we were all in total awe that God had fixed the machine. A few minutes later, Elsie came back in on her own. Apparently, the electrician that came to fix the machine used to be the pastor at her church but had fallen away in his faith. Because of what he had seen out in the garage, he was going to go back to church the following Sunday because he had obviously seen God at work, and who knows what happened after that; he might have gone back into ministry stronger than ever in his faith.

# Chapter Nine

## The Lady with Terminal Cancer

We returned to Fort Worth and met up again with the Bakers, which was great. We were also recommended to attend a particular church where we were assured, we would feel welcome. We didn't want a religious institution that added rules and regulations to the word of God. We truly felt at home in this church and were welcomed with open arms, which was nice. I was invited to join the prison ministry and joined the following week. That experience was like no other, worthy of a book all on its own.

I was also asked if I was interested in volunteering at John Peter Smith Hospital, which I did once a week by taking the book trolley around to the various patients' rooms. They didn't have wards like they do in the UK; instead, they had rooms that held either one, two, three, or four beds in each.

I thoroughly enjoyed both unpaid jobs. I felt that I was giving something back to the community and doing God's work in some way. With the hospital ministry, I would go to John Peter Smith Hospital every Thursday morning around 10 am, check in, get my lanyard with my pass, then get my book trolley and select books I thought people might be interested in, starting from the first floor and working my way up to the sixth floor.

The seventh floor was inhabited by all the people with mental disorders, and above the seventh were all offices, so I wasn't allowed above the sixth. The hospital rooms were laid out like a three-sided cube; in other words, the rooms were on three sides of a square building. I would come out of the lift on each floor and go into each room in turn, working my way around all three sides of that floor before going up to the next floor and so on.

I had been working there on Thursdays for about two months when on one particular day, I reached the sixth floor. I completed the first two sides of the floor, and as I turned the final corner, I could see two very large men dressed all in black standing outside the first door. They looked like a cross between members of the Mafia and two vultures; either way, they looked solemn, so I was expecting the worst.

I pushed my trolley through the two guys into the room where there were another two members of the mob standing against the wall. It was a three-bed room with only one person in the first bed; the others were empty. She was a little old lady, and her husband was sitting by the side of her bed holding her hand.

I was always very bubbly and full of positivity, especially going into rooms where people might be facing surgery or even worse. "Hello, how are you today?" I asked with a big smile. "Not very good today, actually. I have to have an operation in a few minutes." "Oh well, never mind. Can I pray for you? Let's see what God will do about it?" At this, one of the giants said, "You don't need to pray; we're Baptists, we've already prayed." "Well, one more prayer of faith won't hurt, will it?" I said.

At this, the lady and her husband both looked up at me and gave me a half-smile, as if there wasn't any point. I took her hand in mine and prayed an uplifting prayer of faith, giving her a Christian leaflet to read when she comes back from her surgery. I then worked my way along the rest of that side of the building and down to sign out until the next Thursday.

The next Thursday when I arrived at the hospital, something was telling me to start on the sixth floor, not the first floor as usual. It never crossed my mind about the lady from the previous week. I decided to follow the lead inside me and went up to the sixth floor, aiming to work my way down to the first for a change.

Same as the week before, out of the elevator and working my way along the first side of the building, then the second, finally turning the corner to the final corridor. I had forgotten about the two Baptist men who were outside the door the previous week as I entered the room with my trolley and came face to face with the little lady walking toward the door with her husband behind her with her small suitcase.

The moment she saw me, she stopped and smiling a massive smile, she slapped her thigh like she was in a pantomime, saying, "WELL PRAISE GOD, that's why I haven't been able to get out of here all week. God knew that I wanted to say thank you to you." She then went on to tell me that she had terminal cancer and that they were going to try one last time to cut the cancer out of her body.

When she went into surgery a short time after I prayed for her, there was no trace of the cancer in her body, and that God had performed a miracle. She had been trying to leave the hospital for the whole week after her operation and they wouldn't release her.

Then an hour before I arrived, she was told she could shower and get herself ready as they were releasing her. The three of us had the biggest hug there in the room before they left, carrying on with their life and me with my trolley.

God is so good and just because someone thinks that they have a handle on God due to their religious affiliation, that doesn't sway the Lord at all. He responds to faith and a sincere, humble heart. The Bible says in Hebrews 11:6, "Without faith, it is impossible to please God" and also "In everything give thanks, for this is the will of God for you in your life." 1 Thessalonian's 5:18

# Chapter 10

## Linda Summers

I worked as a volunteer at John Peter Smith Hospital for about a year in total. It wasn't a private hospital; it was the equivalent of a National Health Service hospital here in the UK. However, over there, it is classified as a state hospital. So, you might see someone in a bed with a policeman standing next to him and his leg up on a lift because he had been shot in the leg. You never knew from one week to another who or what you would encounter.

I went into a room another week, and again, there was only one person in a bed, although two more beds were empty in the room. The bed was occupied by a lovely-looking lady about 35 years old who was frail and had tubes coming out of her arm. I greeted Linda Summers in my normal buoyant way. After asking what all the tubes were for, she told me that she had Crohn's disease and that she was being fed through the tubes.

I had never even heard of Crohn's disease, and she told me that it was a wasting disease and that she wasn't expected to last much longer. I could see that she was very thin and quite frail but very attractive. I felt so sorry for her and said that I would like to pray for her if she didn't mind. I also spent about 15 minutes explaining God's plan of salvation, and bless her, she gladly bowed her head and prayed a prayer of salvation, asking Jesus to come and live His life in her and through her. I then prayed for her healing and said that I was sure Jesus would heal her, only if she promised to be sitting up the next week without all those tubes coming out of her arm. We smiled at each other, and I left to carry on with my rounds.

When I entered her room the following week, she was sitting up without all the tubes, with another lady about the same age sitting on a chair next to her bed. She greeted me with the sweetest smile, introducing her twin sister who also wanted to meet Jesus, telling me that she was now eating solids and that she would be going to a convalescent home for a few weeks to fully recover. Linda's sister prayed the prayer of salvation just like Linda had the week previously, and I know the day will come when I meet them again, probably in the clouds when Jesus comes back for us. The following week, Linda had left the hospital and there was someone new in the bed she had occupied. How wonderful our Jesus is.

# Chapter 11

## The Little Guy

Years ago in my youth, I used to be a carpet fitter, spending hours on my knees every day and lifting heavy rolls of carpet and rubber underlay as part of the job. When you are young, you don't realize the damage you might be doing to your back, and that is what happened to me. Over the years, I have had many periods of excruciating back pain. When it happens now, I know to go and see a chiropractor. However, in 1989, I hadn't even heard of a chiropractor. So, when I was in serious pain living in Fort Worth, it was natural to go to the emergency department in the same hospital where I was a volunteer, the John Peter Smith Hospital in Fort Worth.

Susan had given birth to our lovely son, Jordan, who was about three months old when my back started to give me a lot of pain. On this particular night, we were just coming back from ministering somewhere when I said I had to go to the emergency department at JPS because my back was giving me a lot of pain. It was about 10:30 at night. Susan and baby Jordan came to wait with me in the terribly busy triage nurse waiting area. I must admit I was very judgemental in those days and when I saw this little old man who was due to go in before me, I judged him as a loud-mouthed alcoholic who wouldn't stop talking. When he went into the triage nurse, he was slurring his words, and everyone could hear what he was saying.

When the nurse had seen him, he came back out into the waiting area, and I was called in for my assessment. I was told I would have to wait to see a doctor, and that there was about an hour and a half wait until I would be seen. On hearing this, I decided to drive Susan and Jordan back home and then return to the hospital. It was now 11:30 pm, and I might be there all night for all I knew.

I returned to the hospital about 12:30, informing the triage nurse of my return. About 1:30, I was called by another nurse and told to follow her to another area. This was an open area with four beds on the left-hand side and four on the right. I was given the second bed from the end on the right-hand side. There was a curtain pulled around the bed on the end, and I could hear someone snoring. I sat on my bed, reading my Ryrie Study Bible, obviously glowing in the dim light because of God's glory all around me (only joking). Not only was I judgemental, but I was also full of pride, taking my Bible everywhere with me so that people knew I was a godly man.

Time went by, and slowly but surely, all the vacant beds became full of people, and I was wondering how much longer I would have to endure the snoring coming from behind the curtain that was getting in the way of my Bible study. A little while later, the snoring stopped, the curtain went back, and the little old man that I had experienced earlier was sitting on the side of his bed. He looked at me and said, "Hi." I responded with a typically English response, "Hello," in my best English accent. I didn't really want to get into a conversation with a drunk, so I went back to reading my Bible.

After a few minutes, he stood up and stretched and said that he needed to pee, stopping a nurse who was walking by to ask where the toilets were. After he had been given directions, he looked at me and said something like, "Wow, she was lovely. I could definitely give her one," except it was more graphic than that, as you can imagine. Me being an ordained minister of the Gospel, got very angry at this sexual outburst and told him that it was disgusting to talk like that and that it had offended me as I was a Christian. At this, he walked off in a bit of a huff in search of the toilet, I guess.

A few minutes later, he returned and came straight up to me and said how sorry he was for offending me with what he said about the nurse. I softened immediately and said that I was a Christian minister and that I didn't like that sort of talk, and neither did God. We then sat down, each on his own bed, looking at each other and started a conversation.

He wanted to know all about me and where in England I was from, and in turn, I found out that he was dyslexic and had managed to work all his life, accumulating enough money to buy a small block of apartments even though he couldn't read or write.

We talked for about 15 minutes, and the conversation came around to where I said about how I became a Christian and that it was all about having Jesus inside our hearts, not just going to church. Spending time with him, I really liked this guy and realized that I had probably misjudged him somewhat.

The conversation came to a place where he allowed me to pray for him to receive Jesus as well as for his dyslexia. We both sat there for a few seconds afterwards with our eyes closed. We opened our eyes, and there was a wonderful peaceful atmosphere, and he looked at my Bible and said, "What sort of Bible is a Ryrie Study Bible anyway?" He looked totally stunned and explained it away by saying that he manages to work out certain words by looking at road signs. He then picked up my Bible, opened it, and it opened at the book of John 1:1, and he started to read, "In the beginning was the Word, and the Word was with God, and the Word was God." He stopped reading and looked at me as he realized that God had touched him in a special way. "I can read! ......I can read....That means I can write too."

He sat there smiling as the realization of what had transpired became more real as the seconds went by. Almost immediately a nurse called for him to go into the doctor, and a few minutes later he came back, and I was called in to see the doctor.

It was now about 4:30 am, and when I had seen the doctor, I came back to my bed, but the little old man had gone. I waited for about 10-15 minutes, until the nurse came out and gave me some tablets which were to help my back. I then left that area and walked toward the exit looking at the large waiting room area that was packed a few hours earlier. Now there were just two people there watching the television, a lady over on the left, and right in front of the TV was the little old man.

I went and sat down next to him, gave him my phone number, and asked him why he was still there. He said he was waiting till 5:30 when his son would have heard the answering machine message so that his son would be able to pick him up. I offered him a lift, and we drove off in the direction of where he lived. It was now about 5:45 am, and as we were driving, he could see his son's car coming toward us. I flashed my lights and pulled up as he got out of the car and crossed the road to his son's car. His parting words were that he would be in touch sometime, then he was gone. About two months later, Susan and I were asleep in bed, and in the middle of the night, the phone by the bed rang. Who could be calling at 2:00 am in the morning? Susan answered the phone and then passed the phone to me saying that it was the little guy from the hospital.

"Hi big fella, I just had to call you, sorry it's late, but I just had to tell you, that I had gangrene in my foot, and they were going to amputate my foot to stop it going up my leg, but God healed that at the same time. I have been telling everyone about Jesus and what He did for me, and one day I'm going to catch you up, I'm telling everyone. See ya big fella."

How wonderful God is, He is always willing and capable of doing more than we need or ask for. I learned a lesson in humility because of that whole episode in the hospital, and I think I became less judgemental in my attitude toward other people thereafter. In Galatians 5:22-26 in the Bible, it talks about the fruit of the Spirit, that's the very character of God, being Love-Joy-Peace-Patience-Kindness-Goodness-Faithfulness-Gentleness, and self-Control. The longer you walk with God, the more He works on you from the inside, changing bad habits and bad attitudes so that things like pride and being judgemental seem to disappear as the fruit develops in your own character.

# Chapter 12

## The Electric Bill

Susan and I were becoming quite popular in our ministry. We would sing some of the songs that we had written in between giving our testimony. I think it was a mixture of us being from the UK with an English accent, Susan's lovely voice, and that our testimony was quite funny, that we were being invited to minister at all sorts of functions.

Women's Aglow was one of these functions. It was a group of Christian ladies that would meet every month, have lunch, and guest speakers would minister to the group of about 40-50 ladies.

Susan and I were what is called "living by faith." We had put our faith totally in the Lord to take care of everything. We were being supported by some people back in the UK who would put a certain amount of money into our bank account every month, which would normally pay for things like the utility bill that had to be paid. I can't remember exactly how it worked, but the post office was involved in the transfer of funds to our bank account in the US every month. However, the post office had gone on strike in the UK, and there was nothing sent over to our bank account for a few weeks. It didn't really bother us as we had food and a full tank of gas in the Oldsmobile to get us around.

The only thing was, we had a utility bill of $335 that needed to be paid by 4:00 pm this day or they were going to cut the power off. It was already a couple of weeks overdue, and they don't mess about over there.

We arrived at the Women's Aglow location, which was being held in a cafeteria in Fort Worth, set up the microphone, etc.. and started to deliver our usual ministry. At the end of our ministering to these lovely ladies, we received a wonderful ovation, which was great, and I left the little stage to go to the restroom as a lady called Gloria stood up and said in her Texan drawl, "I think we should do a special collection for the Oxbrows to say thank you for their wonderful ministry." Now, this was nice to hear as we always did our ministering without charge. It was always a blessing to do God's work, and anyway, He was taking care of everything.

While I was in the restroom, I took a couple of minutes to pray a prayer of thanks for how we had been received and that they were doing a special collection for us. I came back into where all the ladies were and joined Susan, who was speaking to several ladies who wanted to speak with us personally. A few minutes later, the lady who was the organizer of the WA meeting called me to one side and said how pleasantly surprised she was because normally when they do a collection for the people who minister, the ladies don't normally give more than $50, but this time they had given just over $335. I took Susan off to one side and told her how much we had been blessed with, and that I would go off and pay the electric bill and would she ask one of the ladies to drop her and Jordan off at home. Once again, God had proved that He had us in the palm of His hand. If it had been, let's say $100 or even $200, it would have been generous, but to get the almost exact amount to the dollar could only have been God.

# Chapter 13

## Jessie Rocha

About a week after the Women's Aglow meeting, I answered a call on the home phone from a man named Jessie Rocha, who spoke with a strong Mexican/Texan accent. During our conversation, he explained that his wife had attended the WA meeting and had brought the tape recording from that day. He wondered if we would be willing to come and give our testimony at a special event held by his college once a year on Valentine's Day, in a hotel for people just starting out in their new careers and relationships.

I expressed how much we would love to do that but mentioned that I didn't have a car at the time as it was in for repairs. He kindly offered to pick us up and take us to the venue if I provided him with our address. He then inquired about our fee, to which I responded that it is a pleasure to share what God has done in our lives and that we wouldn't dream of charging a cent.

After giving Jessie our address and arranging the time and day for pick-up, which was about a week away, we exchanged goodbyes and hung up. It was an honour to convey that it would be a blessing for us to minister free of charge. In the USA, such gestures are uncommon; people seem to charge for everything.

A couple of days later, around 6 pm, after spending the day helping Micky at his RV dealership, I arrived home. Susan was about to serve my dinner as I only had a few minutes before being picked up by a church member who was also involved in the prison ministry.

The phone rang, and I picked it up to find Jessie Rocha on the other end. "Hello Rodney, it's Jessie," he said. "I just wanted to confirm your address for when I pick you up." At that time, phones had a cable of about 20 feet, allowing you to move around your apartment while talking.

I walked over to the window and described our surroundings to Jessie. "If I were looking out of my window now, I would be overlooking the car park in the apartments, with Minyards and Walmart to the right," I said. "Are you standing by your window now, Rodney?" he asked. I confirmed, and he said he was outside in his car, flashing his headlights.

He asked if he could come up, and I welcomed him, mentioning that I was about to leave in a few minutes but suggested he join us for coffee. Susan brought Jessie a cup of coffee while I quickly ate my dinner. Out of the corner of my eye, I noticed Jessie seemed a bit fidgety, and suddenly, he reached into his inside jacket pocket, pulled out a check book and pen, and began writing my name on it.

With a slight tremble, he explained that God had woken him up in the middle of the night, instructing him to give me a cheque for $500. He recounted how he went to the kitchen, still uncertain about what had happened, when his wife came in, saying that God had woken her up and told her to tell him to write me a cheque for $500. He assured me that it had to be God's doing, as he had never written a cheque for this amount before.

I finished my dinner, expressing my gratitude to Jessie before leaving him with Susan as my ride had honked the horn outside, indicating he was waiting for me. We were still waiting for money to come from the UK at that time, so the $500 was much needed for various expenses. Once again, God provided.

As I write these accounts, they deeply move me emotionally. Tears of joy fill my eyes as I recall the wonderful things God has done in my life. These cannot be mere coincidences; they are undoubtedly God-incidences, and I hope you agree as you read them.

# Chapter 14

## The Synagogue in Dallas

Micky and Twilight were still very active in our lives and had been since our third day in Texas, which was great. One day, Micky said that he wanted to invite Susan and I to a special Yom Kippur event at his synagogue in Dallas. Micky was like so many people who classify themselves as Christians by going to church at Christmas time or Easter or if there is a funeral or a wedding but at no other time.

However, it was a wonderful thing to be invited, and I gladly accepted the invitation on behalf of Susan and myself and arranged with Clayton to babysit Jordan. It was a posh do, so Susan and I were suited and booted as they say. Micky was going to pick us up at about 5:30, allowing loads of time for us all to get to the synagogue in Dallas before the start at 7:00 PM.

5:30 came and went, as did 5:45, with Micky pulling up outside our apartment in the green Rolls Royce a couple of minutes before 6:00 pm. Susan made her way down to the car, and I was about to leave when, for some reason, something said for me to pick up the little ringed notepad. This was a small notepad about half the size of an envelope with a pen that fitted in the wire on the edge.

Anyway, for whatever reason, I picked it up and put it in the inside pocket of my suit. I went down to the car only to find out that I was going to be driving the Rolls, which was a treat for me. We finally pulled up outside the synagogue about 10 minutes past 7:00 pm. I let Micky, Twilight, and Susan out of the car and then drove off to park it. When I got back to the outside of the synagogue a couple of minutes later, the three of them were standing on the steps. This was a really well to do place; it had its own little ticket window with the cost of a ticket $25 on the window, it was just like buying a ticket to the theatre, however, the screen had been pulled down with "sold out" on the window.

Micky had failed to buy the necessary tickets, and we were too late to get in anyway 😞. We were standing there wondering what we were to do next. Do we go for a meal now? When suddenly a door opened, with a security usher guy coming out and saying, "You're lucky there are four seats left up in the gallery but to hurry." We thanked him and all started to ascend the stairs to the gallery; we didn't even have to pay for a ticket 😊.

We came through the closed door into the theatre-type part of the building, and I could tell immediately that this was a very elegant place, lots of red and gold, very plush indeed. On the left as we came in, there were two ladies, one playing the cello and the other playing a violin, which was nice.

Another usher came up to us immediately and said, "Hurry up, it's about to start, there are two seats here and another two along there." All four seats were right in the front row; two of them were about 20 seats further along from the side where we were standing. Micky and Twilight started to work their way along the row to their seats. Our two seats were seat 3 and 4 on the first row, and

I, as a gentleman, let Susan go in first past the exceptionally large gentleman on the end and his very large partner next to him who was then sitting next to me.

We took our seats, and everything started immediately, with the two ladies finishing their musical interlude and people coming out on the stage part of the building many feet below. I had been in a synagogue many years before, but it was nothing like this; it was like being in the London Palladium, but the seating was all banked up, with no space between each row and very, very steep indeed. Anyway, it was great to be there, and I was just pleased that it hadn't been a wasted trip.

A few minutes later, a man came and got the two rolls of the Torah from a gold-type cabinet and brought them forward to the front part of the stage. It was then that I heard the voice of God inside me. "Rodney, I want you to be obedient to me. I want you to take out the notebook from your inside pocket." I must admit it came as a surprise to me, especially as we were in a Jewish synagogue, so I totally ignored the voice, putting it down to my imagination.

"Rodney, I want you to be obedient to me, I want you to take out the notebook from your inside pocket." Okay, so maybe the Lord wanted me to make a note of something, so I took out the notebook and sat there with it on my lap waiting for whatever He wanted me to take note of. Then it happened again. "Rodney, I want you to be obedient to me, I want you to take the pen and open the notebook and write in big letters the word JESUS."

Well, now I started to get fidgety. "Lord, I'm in a synagogue, you know," I said on the inside to the voice. I looked behind me, and all the people there were Hasidic Jews, and the seats were banked so steeply that the guy behind me could easily see what I was writing without having to lean forward. Then it came again. "Rodney, I want you to be obedient to me. Take out the notebook and write in big letters the word JESUS."

So, I opened it up, and wrote JESUS in nice big letters, closed the notebook again, and sat there feeling pleased with myself because I had carried out the test by the Lord. I got a funny look from Susan, much as to say, "What are you up to this time?" But I just kept looking forward trying to understand everything that was going on.

Then the voice came again. "Rodney, I want you to be obedient to me, open up the notebook and under the name Jesus, I want you to write in big letters IS ALIVE." Now, I really was squirming in my seat; I didn't feel relaxed at all. But the voice came again and repeated the instruction. So, reluctantly, I opened the notebook and wrote in big letters IS ALIVE. I closed the book and put it back in my inside pocket because I had done what the Lord wanted.

Five minutes or so went by before the voice spoke again. "Rodney, I want you to be obedient to me, I want you to take out the notebook and tear out the page with Jesus is alive written on it and fold it up." At this point, one thing started going through my mind. I looked over the balcony at the hundreds of people below and thought how the religious guys behind me might delight in throwing me off the balcony, and how easy it was for them to see everything I was doing.

"Rodney, I want you to be obedient to me, I want you to take out the notebook and tear out the page with Jesus is alive written on it and fold it up."

So again, I was obedient and took out the notebook from my jacket, opened up the page, and decided to tear out the page slowly. However, because it had that wire spindle thing, as I tore the page out slowly, it made a slow popping sound which was at a quiet moment in the proceedings. I could feel the eyes behind me overseeing everything I was doing, and it was very unnerving indeed.

I folded up the page and put the notebook and pen back in my pocket and just sat there wondering what was next. Susan's face was classic as she knew something was happening but didn't know what. All this had taken about 40 minutes since we first sat down. I just sat there feeling good that I had done it all even if it hadn't been God, even if the devil was trying to get me thrown off the edge, I had overcome it all.

Then it happened again, Oh no!!!!! "Rodney, I want you to be obedient to me. When I tell you, I want you to give the sheet of paper to the lady on your left."

Now it was serious, what do I do? I looked at the lady on my left who also saw all what I was doing and then I looked at her husband who was massive. I just sat there stunned, then Susan asked me what I was doing and why I was fidgeting? I whispered to her what God had told me to do and she assured me that it could not have been God because He would have given her the job of giving it to the woman, not me. This did not help me at all.

My mind was in turmoil now, I really did not know what to do. The rabbi had started to give his speech a few minutes earlier, so I decided to be clever. I said to the voice inside, "If this is really you God, you will get the Rabbi to mention the name of Jesus in his sermon." Now I was on safe ground. If it was the devil he couldn't do it, if it was my mind playing up it wouldn't happen, and if it is God the Rabbi will certainly say the name of Jesus for sure.

I sat there content that it was a safe bet and that I wouldn't have to do anything else. When suddenly, the Rabbi said, "Some people think the Messiah has already been and that His name is Jesus." I can't remember the rest of what he was saying because I was in total shock. It obviously was God all the time, in a synagogue of all places.

The Rabbi finished his sermon, then something else was said by someone on the stage and suddenly it was over. That is when I heard for the last time "Rodney, give the paper to the lady now." Everyone was standing up and getting ready to leave, so I stood up and turned to the lady on my left and said, "Hi, I really think that God wanted me to give this to you."

I turned and faced Susan straight away, helping her put on her coat, mainly because I was expecting a punch or something coming from the massive husband. I could see Micky and Twilight working their way along the row when I got a tap on the shoulder. "Excuse me" …. I ignored it…. "Excuse me." This time I had to turn, and it was the lady and her fella both smiling at me. She did give me her name, but I cannot for the life of me remember what it was, but she said that she and her fiancé Mr. Mendelssohn were trying to decide which faith to follow and that he was Jewish, and she was a Baptist. They had decided that they would visit one place of worship then the other, to then decide which faith to follow. I think God showed which way to go.

Micky and Twilight were totally amazed at what had transpired and the six of us stood outside the synagogue for a long time after it had closed just talking. Mr. Mendelssohn was someone important in AT&T, I remember that, but I don't know if Micky kept in touch with them, but I didn't. In 1 Kings 19:11-13, it talks about the still small voice, which is the voice of the Lord talking to you on the inside. You could be in the middle of an earthquake, a football match, a concert, or even a synagogue like with me, and God can talk to you.

I'm pleased to say that I have heard His voice many times in my life and hope to hear it many more times. Hopefully, I get to hear Him say "Well done, my good and faithful servant." Matthew 25:21.

# Chapter 15

## Two £5 Notes

As I stated right at the beginning, sometimes you witness something totally miraculous, like a leg growing, and at other times it might just be a little touch of love from the Father that answers a need you have. After our return from the USA, Susan and I lived in Cricklewood for a period, and things were a bit tight financially. Actually, we were broke, and I didn't know how to buy some things I needed like food. We had the two of us to feed, as well as Jordan, who was about three. We had also been given a Great Dane dog, Mimi, by friends in our church at that time. We were living in Gladstone Park Gardens, and right at the bottom of the road was Gladstone Park itself, where I would take Mimi for her walks of a day. I really loved taking Mimi out to the park, especially at night-time when it was quiet, and I could enjoy some quiet time.

This particular evening about 9:00 p.m. and raining heavily, not the most enjoyable time to walk the dog, but it had to be done. I dressed up in my foul weather gear, put Mimi's collar on her, and started the walk down to the park. As I reached the open gate, just before letting Mimi off her lead, I looked to the right-hand side of the entrance and saw two £5 notes just sitting there. That was amazing in itself as I really needed £10 at the time, but what was really incredible was that both of the £5 notes were totally bone dry. It was pouring down with rain, no one else was around, and it was as if an Angel had just laid them there a few seconds before I arrived. Even then, you would expect them to have had a few drops of rain on them, but no, there was nothing. That was in the early 90s, and £10 would buy a lot more then than it would now. It really was God's provision for us. One of the names of God in the Old Testament is Jehovah Jireh, meaning the Lord God who is our provider. He proved that He could take care of my needs that evening.

# Chapter 16

## The IRA

During 1992, I was a milkman in the Cricklewood area of London. I did this job for about 6 months in total which was long enough quite honestly. At the time of writing this, milkmen and the little milk floats have disappeared from our streets, but going back to the 1990s it was quite normal to see little electric three-wheeler milk floats on the streets delivering milk round the houses; this is when milk came in glass bottles as opposed to 1-liter plastic containers that you buy nowadays from the supermarket. It was a hard job, demanding that you start very early of a day in order to get the milk delivered to the 220 different houses, etc. that were on your round.

This particular day, I arrived at the milk depot in Cricklewood at 4:00 am, loaded up my milk float with all the milk, eggs, bacon, and bread that needed to be delivered and left the depot in the dark heading to my first drop, a small block of old people flats about a mile away. I don't know if the reader has ever travelled around the city first thing in the morning, but it is a time when people who might have been working during the night are rushing to finish their work and get home, and people such as milkmen and bread delivery people, etc.. are trying to get as much done before the traffic starts to build up.

So, when you see a vehicle doing about 29 miles an hour in a 30 mph area, it sticks out like a sore thumb. I pulled up outside the small block of flats and as I was loading up my milk bottle carrier in the dark, I looked to the left and noticed a 30 hundredweight van going by. However, this was different, there were no markings on the sides, it was going under 30 mph as if not to be noticed by the police, and the driver looked exactly like Barry McGuigan, the Irish world champion boxer. I'm not saying it was him, but this guy was his spitting image. He had his window down and as we looked at each other something set off an alarm inside me. His vehicle going by was almost like a film in slow motion, with the two of us staring at each other until his van had passed me.

At that time in mainland England, there was a campaign of terror bombings by the IRA, the Irish Republican Army. If the reader is of an age, he or she will remember how London was on high alert because there could be a nail bomb in a rubbish bin or in the boot of a car that would be set off remotely by one of the members of the IRA, as on July 20th, 1982, when they set off two bombs, one in Hyde Park and the other in Regents Park in London, killing 11 military personnel, 7 horses in Hyde Park and 7 members of a military band and dozens of civilians being seriously injured. I instinctively knew that the Barry McGuigan lookalike was a member of the IRA and was going to do something evil.

The Bible talks about Christians having discernment of spirits, to tell the difference between good and evil and I knew on the inside of me that this was an evil thing that was going to happen. My insides were sort of churning; I was totally uneasy and very concerned. However, I still had a lot of milk to deliver, so I decided that I would carry on with my normal milk round and tell everything to the first policeman I saw that morning.

It was about 8:15 that morning before I saw a member of the constabulary; it was a sergeant who was standing outside a shop. I pulled my three-wheeler to the side of the road and went to tell him my experience. His response was shocking; he treated me like I was a little boy. "So let me get this right, you have seen a very nasty man who was driving a big van, and you are sure he is going to do something very, very naughty, but you didn't get the number that is on his van so that we could find him. Is that right?" Obviously, I wasn't taken seriously at all, so all I could do was carry on with my deliveries. I got back to the milk depot about 2:15 in the afternoon and as soon as I drove in, two guys came running up to me asking if I had heard about the Wood Green Shopping Centre being bombed. It was of great interest and concern to them as it was only a 10-minute drive from the milk depot and suddenly everyone was on high alert.

When I got home later that afternoon, I decided to call the Special Branch and give them my account of what I had seen. The response from the lady on the phone wasn't as bad as the police sergeant earlier in the day, but very similar. I was assured that I would get a phone call within the next few days to clarify what I had told her, and that was it, the end of the call. A week went by, and I still hadn't had the phone call from Special Branch, so I called them again. This time I was assured that I would get a call, but that they were very busy following up on leads they had received. Consequently, I decided to leave it for them to contact me when they were ready.

About two months went by and I was about to take Mimi out for her nightly walk in Gladstone Park when Susan stopped me outside the house and asked me if I could go up to the garage and get some milk as we didn't have enough for the morning. So instead of turning left out the front of my house, I had to turn right and go up to the busy Cricklewood Broadway. It was about 9:00 pm and as usual, there was a lot of traffic on the Broadway. I got to the top of my road and used the Zebra crossing to get to the other side of the road where the garage was. Unfortunately, they had sold out of milk which meant that I had to walk further along the Broadway to another garage to see if they had milk.

As Mimi and I were walking, a white Ford Transit van was driving slowly along the other side of the road; I didn't pay much attention to this mainly because Mimi was such a striking looking dog, her grandfather had won Crufts dog show a number of years before and it was a regular occurrence for people to take a good look at her.

The next garage had also sold out of milk, which meant that I had to cross the road and go to the last of the three garages down on the left-hand side of The Broadway. Wonderful, they had milk so all I had to do was take it back to my house and then I could get to the park. As we were walking back towards Gladstone Park Gardens, a white Ford Transit van went slowly along the same direction as we were walking. This time I thought it was a little alarming, I didn't know if it was the same van as a few minutes earlier, it was dark, I couldn't see who was driving the van and anyway I might be imagining things.

On the 7th of February 1991, the IRA had tried to kill the then Prime Minister John Major, by firing a mortar bomb out of the top of a white Ford Transit van, and this was still fresh in my mind. So, I wasn't greatly alarmed, but I was aware of the situation with the inquisitive van driver. I decided that when I turned into my road, I would quickly walk left into where there was a block of flats. I would wait there for a couple of minutes and if the van didn't show up then I was obviously being concerned over nothing, and if the van did come into the area, I would know that this was then serious.

Mimi and I stood against a wall in an unlit area of the car park, Mimi looking up at me as if to say I thought we were going to the park, not standing against walls all night. Phew what a relief, I waited there for about 2 minutes and there was no sign of the van, so Mimi and I started to walk out of the area back onto Gladstone Park Gardens, but just as we were about to reach the road, the white van drove in. Now it was serious, my heart was beating faster than it had ever beaten before. I had to think quickly what to do. If it was the guy from the IRA, he may have been given some of my information by an IRA sympathizer working at the special branch, like the name of the road but not the number.

Also, Cricklewood is a very Irish area, and the IRA guy may have just been driving along the road and saw me, who knows? So, now I had to walk to my house, give Susan the milk and then walk down to the park with Mimi, all without this guy finding out what number I lived at.

Mimi and I walked at a great pace to get to my front door as quickly as I could and as I got nearer to my house the white van came past me again, stopping about 100 yards down on the right-hand side. I knocked on the door as I hadn't taken my house keys, Susan came to the door and as I was trying to get her to take the milk and go inside, the white van is turning around and coming back up towards where I was. The van slowed down, and the Barry McGuigan lookalike was pulling up slowly the other side of the road with his window down.

The old Rodney of my youth started to take over, I wanted to punch this guy, I was angry. He stopped his van and was looking at me just like he had done a few months earlier. "Are you looking for me?" I said. "Why should I be looking for you then?" he said in a distinctive Northern Irish accent. "Because I'm here if you want me." I was shaking with anger, this guy by being there, was a threat to me and my family and I so wanted to drag him out of his van and hit him so badly. "Oh, that's good then, so if I need you, I know where you are. Well, I'll be on my way then, so I might see you again." With that, he drove off and turned left into the next street and disappeared. Susan in her normal supportive way, thought that I was imagining everything and was just picking on some poor guy driving by.

Shaking with anger and fear, I decided to tell her later and continued down the road toward the park to finally give Mimi her evening walk. As I reached the bottom of the road and started to cross over and go through the open gate where the two £5 notes were laying on a previous occasion, I could see that the Irish guy had indeed turned left into the other road but had also come down to the entrance of the park. The same van was sitting there with the engine running and lights off.

Mimi and I went into the park, and I let her off the leash to have her run around. It was pitch black and as I looked toward the van, I could see the burning end of a cigarette glowing every time the driver took a puff of it. I didn't go into the blackness of the park; I stayed on the path near the road with just trees and hedges between me and the man.

I thought if he wants to shoot me that would be better than him and others with him, coming into my house in the middle of the night and killing me, Susan, and Jordan too, my little boy. The IRA had a reputation of doing that sort of thing over in Ireland and I just did not know what to expect. Mimi executed her nightly routine of disappearing into the darkness of the park and coming back after she had done her business. We walked down the path to an exit further along the same road the van was in.

I put Mimi back on her leash and stood behind a workman's cabin that was sitting in the road near the exit. I kept peeking around the back of the cabin at the van and after a couple of minutes, he put the lights on and turned the van around and drove off. I was pleased, but aware that he might just come back in the middle of the night and do who knows what? I went back home and explained everything to Susan who took it all with a pinch of salt as if she did not really believe any of it.

It was now quite late and making sure everything was locked up for the night, Susan and I went to bed. She went to sleep almost straight away; however, my mind was going over everything that had happened which was preventing me from getting any sleep. Gladstone Park Gardens is what is known as a rat run, cars use it as a fast cut through to get to Cricklewood Broadway, so every minute or so there was the sound of a vehicle coming along the road and every time I heard something, I was thinking that the guy or guys were going to come in and kill us. Because I was restless, this woke Susan up who told me to forget it and go to sleep, but I just couldn't. She woke up again about 15 minutes later and said that she was now quite concerned and that she couldn't sleep either.

I was just lying there with my mind playing out all the different scenarios when suddenly I heard the voice of God once again on the inside obviously. And we had a conversation in my mind, although it was a very real and loud conversation. The following is almost word for word. "What are you doing Rodney?" "Lord, you saw the guy, you know what the IRA are like." "Rodney let's talk about your life. Are you trusting in Me for anything?" "Well yes Lord, I'm trusting in you for everything." "Like what?" "Well, our food, my family and my eternal life in particular." "Rodney, is your Eternal Life a big thing?" "Yes Lord, it's the biggest thing." "Are you trusting in yourself for any of those things?" "No Lord, it's all You, I cannot do anything." "Well then Rodney trust me in this, no one can harm you unless I say it is okay."

At this point, an incredible sensation of peace came over me and I was asleep within 10 seconds and I can honestly say that was the last time I worried about anything. I have had a lot of opportunities to worry because of life itself is not easy sometimes, but I have learned to do what the Bible says, to roll all my cares over to Him. It says in Philippians 4:6 "Do not be anxious about anything, but in every situation, by prayer and petition, with thanksgiving, present your requests to God." And what is amazing is, it works.

I did get a phone call sometime later from the Special Branch who said that they had reason to believe that my account and description were accurate and that I would get another phone call asking me to have a look at some photos. However, I am still waiting for that call, and they still haven't arrested anyone for the bombing. Oh well.

# Chapter 17

## Looking for my Father

I was having a discussion with a man in church about certain things in the Bible, and he asked if he and his son could come around sometime and do a Bible study with me. This spread quite quickly, and three months later we had 32 people, many from different churches around London, coming to our house every Thursday evening, and it was the highlight of everyone's week, including mine. Some of these were people that wouldn't have entered a normal church setting for whatever reason, and it was great to see God answer prayers for so many of them and to see them grow in their faith.

My parents split up when I was two years old, so I didn't know my father at all, but there was a desire to find out about him and maybe even meet him if he was still alive. I know the Mormon church, and I think the Salvation Army have a finding service, but I decided to bring it before all the people on a Thursday evening and have us all pray about it and see what God would do.

I explained my desire to everyone on Thursday, and we all prayed in agreement that God would work a miracle in my life and help me in my search. I was working in finance at this time as an investment consultant; really, I sold insurance, but the job title on the business card was investment consultant, so I would sometimes travel miles to see someone who was interested in taking out a savings plan, pension, or insurance.

The day following the house church prayers, I had an appointment in Leighton Buzzard a little bit north of my home-town of Luton. This was in the days prior to mobile phones, so before I arrived at the appointment, I stopped at a call box and phoned my office to see if they had managed to confirm the appointment. However, the person had cancelled the arranged meeting, so I had some time free before my next appointment back in London.

The company I was working for during this time was advertising with leaflets in various places, one of which was Luton airport, so I decided to travel back to London via Stopsley north of Luton and top up the display at the airport. I drove through Stopsley and was on the dual carriageway toward the airport when I heard that still small voice inside saying Putteridge Road, Putteridge Road. I suddenly remembered; my grandfather used to live in Putteridge Road. At the next opportunity, I headed back to the large roundabout in Stopsley and slowly looked at the names of the roads that branched off, and sure enough, one of them was indeed Putteridge Road, although I hadn't noticed it when I was on the roundabout 5 minutes earlier. I entered Putteridge Road and parked outside the first house on the left.

My heart was beating faster than normal at this point, and I decided to knock on the first house and ask if they had any knowledge of my dad, Percy Gilbert. A lady answered the door of the first house, suggesting I ask at the house next door to her as she had only lived there a couple of months. It took a while for the man next door to answer the door as he was very old and couldn't walk very easily, but when I asked him, he said, "Is he a little guy?" "Yes, my mum and dad were both under 5ft" "Well, there's a little guy who's lived in the street for donkey's years, it might be him. You see that house with the red roof, it's either that one or the one before it, he lives there."

Now my heart was beating even faster than before. I drove down the road and stopped outside the house with the red roof but decided to go into the paper shop opposite and ask as he might have papers delivered. The Indian guy who ran the shop didn't know of Percy Gilbert, so I decided to knock on the door with the red roof and hope. A young guy about 11 answered the door, and his mother was walking up behind him when I asked the same question. "Is he a little guy, because I think he lives next door." As I walked up the pathway to the house next door, I was expecting Cilia Black to suddenly jump out saying "Surprise Surprise!" like in her TV program.

I took a deep breath and knocked on the door; it was answered by a lovely smiling lady who opened the door as wide as her smile and asked if she could help me. "Yes, thank you, I'm looking for Percy Gilbert." As I said this, I could see my father coming down the stairs, then standing in front of me looking up at my face wondering who I was and what I wanted. I think Ann, his wife who answered the door, put two and two together and realized who I was, saying "you'll have to tell him who you are love, his eyesight isn't that good nowadays. " "Hi dad, I'm Rodney, your son." He almost collapsed when I said this "Rodney, ………….. I thought you were dead!" He then put his arms up to hold me, and we hugged for about a minute, maybe more. "Your father is the loveliest man that ever walked the earth," Ann said.

I spent about an hour drinking tea, looking at old photos and basically just catching up with what had happened over the past 40 something years. We then arranged a day when I would come back with Susan and Jordan to also meet other members of the family that I hadn't met before. Driving back to London I couldn't help but think just how totally awesome God was, it was less than 24 hours since we all prayed, and He had again proved just how big He is and how much He cares about His children.

I did go back with Susan and Jordan; we had a few hours there. Bless them, they laid on all sorts of sandwiches and drinks for us which was nice, but that was the last time either of us were in contact with each other. I think we both realized that we were in two different worlds. God had answered my prayer and satisfied the question of what had happened to me for my dad at the same time.

# Chapter 18

## The beach in Australia

Miracles are not necessarily seeing God part the Red Sea or raising someone from the dead; sometimes they may be very personal, and to the world, they might appear very small. But it is often the small things that God does that proves just how big He is. As I mentioned at the beginning of this book, this is in no way an exhaustive account of the incredible things I have been blessed to see and experience in my life. I wish to end this book though with two accounts that are very special to me. Both occurred while I was living in Port Macquarie in NSW, Australia, where I lived for 9 years. It was my pleasure and joy to walk along the 14-mile beach between Port Macquarie and Lake Cathie. I only ever managed to walk the full distance once, but always managed to enjoy a few good miles of beautiful sands daily, 32 degrees, and pods of dolphins in the waves coming into shore, to me it was paradise.

One day I was at least three miles along the beach, and there was no one else walking in either direction as far as you could see, and this was my ideal time to be out with the Creator of the Universe and have my prayer time with Him. As I was walking along the sand, kicking the waves as they rushed in and covered my footprints, I suddenly saw a wristwatch. I picked it up, and sure enough, it was working, even showing the correct time. The strap was quite worn away, but the watch itself was working great. I looked around to see who the owner of it could be. As I said, there was no one on the beach for miles in either direction, so it had to be someone in the water, maybe a swimmer, but there was no one anywhere.

It was then that I heard the voice of God again inside of me saying, "You have found time… You have found time to pray, you have found time to be with me. You have found time." How amazing that was. There have been times when I have looked around to see where the voice might be coming from as it was so loud, only to realize that there was no one near and that it could only be on the inside. You can see a photo of the wristwatch on the cover of this book; I keep it by my bed although I haven't put a battery in it since it stopped a few years ago.

There was another time I was walking along the same stretch of beach, but this was at a time when I really needed to decide about which direction of my life I should take. I really needed to hear from God, and my mind was clouded with the different possibilities in front of me, and I just wasn't hearing His voice.

For a period of months, I would spend time every day walking the beach praying and looking for pebbles. Not just any pebble, it had to be a certain size and beautiful. Some pebbles are like outer space when you look at them, some are just plain, but if you hunt for them, some are quite exquisite with beautiful colours and patterns. I had collected a number of these pebbles and wanted to have them varnished and laid out on the top of a table. However, I was always looking for a larger pebble with a cross on it to put in the centre of the table with all the other pebbles surrounding it, but I could never find one. It probably was a little bit too much to ask for, but I kept looking for weeks on end.

There was a Godly man in the Old Testament called Gideon. Gideon was famous for a few things but in particular he needed to hear from heaven as to what to do in a certain situation. So he laid a fleece on the threshing floor and said that if he gets up in the morning and the fleece is wet but the floor around the fleece is dry, he will know that God is saying to do this particular thing. So, in the morning, he sees that the fleece is wet but the floor around the fleece is totally dry. But then he laid another fleece to be certain that it was God. This time it was the reverse; he wanted to get up in the morning and the fleece be totally dry and the surrounding threshing floor be totally wet, which it was.

Going back to my situation, there were two possible directions for my life to take, one more pleasant than the other. I won't elaborate here, but one direction involved giving something up which I didn't want to do, but I still wanted to be in God's will. The other direction was less challenging. So, I am walking on the beach this beautiful day, looking for the impossible pebble with a cross and talking to God at the same time. Picking up a pebble here and throwing it down again, then picking up another one with the same result, like I had done a thousand times before. I was also talking to God and saying about the decision I had to make. In the distance, I could see a woman running toward me, which was rare this far out of Port Macquarie. I then decided I would be clever; I would lay a fleece just like Gideon in the Bible, but I would make it so that the odds were on my side if you understand what I mean. OK Lord if you want me to go in this direction, you will give me a pebble with a cross on it.

How clever was I 😊 ... However, not 10 seconds went by before I saw the pebble right in front of me, I picked it up and couldn't believe it. The lady was almost right in front of me now, and I said to her "excuse me", she took the hearing pods out of her ears and asked me to repeat what I said, "Excuse me, sorry for troubling you, but can you see anything unusual about this pebble?" "Apart from the cross you mean?" I thanked her, and she continued to run on. I was totally in awe, I walked back along the beach toward Port Macquarie confident in the path my life should take, which as it turned out was wonderful.

I kept looking at the pebble, and it was then that I realized that as well as the cross, there was the outline of Jesus with the sudarium, His head covering on the side of the cross. It just reaffirmed everything to me. You can see a picture of the pebble on the cover of this book as well as the watch, see if you can see Jesus as well as the cross. I keep the pebble beside my bed as well as the watch as a constant reminder of His love and care for me in my life.

# Conclusion

I have shared a few of the experiences I have enjoyed in 40 plus years; however, there are more things that I have seen and experienced than I can possibly recall or write down. One of the greatest miracles that happens throughout the world daily is when a person is raised from death into life. Seeing someone who is spiritually dead accept the life of Jesus to live His life in them and through them is a true miracle.

I have seen many people pray a prayer of salvation, asking Jesus for His life, and minutes later see a completely different person standing in front of me. Often all the stress of the world seems to drain out of them, and a feeling of peace and joy comes in.
If the reader has never considered asking for His eternal life, maybe today is the ideal day to experience your own miracle; there is nothing to lose and everything to gain.

I would like to say a big thank you for buying this book; I hope and believe it has been a blessing to you. I have said many times especially recently with the world being in turmoil like it is, I don't know how people can go from day to day without having God in their lives. If you have never come to a place where you give God control of your life, can I ask you to consider it? I have met people who say if He is real, let Him show me only then will I believe, but the way it works is if you believe, He will then show you.

May the Grace of our Lord Jesus Christ, the love of God the Father, and the fellowship of the Holy Spirit be with you from this moment on.

With His love and in His service,
Rodney


Should you wish to contact me at any time, you can email me on.

Roxbrow2024@gmail.com

www.ingramcontent.com/pod-product-compliance
Lightning Source LLC
Chambersburg PA
CBHW070332120526
44590CB00017B/2856